CONAMARA BLUES

Also by John O'Donohue

ANAM CARA
ETERNAL ECHOES
ECHOES OF MEMORY
PERSON ALS VERMITTLUNG
DIVINE BEAUTY
BENEDICTUS

CONAMARA BLUES

JOHN O'DONOHUE

BANTAM BOOKS
SYDNEY • AUCKLAND • TORONTO • NEW YORK • LONDON

CONAMARA BLUES
A BANTAM BOOK : 9780553813227

Originally published in Great Britain by Doubleday,
a division of Transworld Publishers

PRINTING HISTORY
Doubleday edition published 2000
Bantam Books edition published 2001

10

Typeset 12 on 16pt Granjon by Julia Lloyd.

Bantam Books are published by Transworld Publishers,
61–63 Uxbridge Road, London W5 5SA,
A Random House Group Company.

Addresses for Random House Group Ltd companies outside the UK
can be found at: www.randomhouse.co.uk
The Random House Group Ltd Reg. No. 954009.

The Random House Group Limited supports The Forest Stewardship
Council® (FSC®), the leading international forest-certification organisation.
Our books carrying the FSC label are printed on FSC®-certified paper.
FSC is the only forest-certification scheme supported by the leading
environmental organisations, including Greenpeace. Our
paper procurement policy can be found at
www.randomhouse.co.uk/environment

Printed and bound in Great Britain by Clays Ltd, St Ives plc

In memory of my aunt
MARY O'DONOHUE
(1896–1923)
from Caherbeanna who died in a tragic
road accident shortly after her
emigration to America

Contents

1 APPROACHINGS

2 ENCOUNTERS:
THE ROSARY SONNETS

THE JOYFUL MYSTERIES

THE SORROWFUL MYSTERIES

THE GLORIOUS MYSTERIES

CONAMARA BLUES

ONE
APPROACHINGS

'I want to watch watching arrive.
I want to watch arrivances.'

HELENE CIXOUS

'I think back gladly on the future.'

HANS MAGNUS ENZENSBERGER

'Think of things that disappear.

Think of what you love best,
what brings tears into your eyes.

Something that said *adios* to you
before you knew what it meant
or how long it was for.'

NAOMI SHIHAB NYE

Before the Beginning

Unknown to us, there are moments
When crevices we cannot see open
For time to come alive with beginning.

As in autumn a field of corn
Knows when enough green has been inhaled
From the clay and under the skill
Of an artist breeze becomes gold in a day,

When the ocean still as a mirror
Of a sudden takes a sinister turn
To rise in a mountain of wave
That would swallow a village.

How to a flock of starlings
Scattered, at work on grass,
From somewhere, a signal comes
And suddenly as one, they describe
A geometric shape in the air.

When the audience becomes still
And the soprano lets the silence deepen,
In that slowed holding, the whole aria
Hovers nearer, then alights

On the wings of breath
Poised to soar into song.

These inklings were first prescribed
The morning we met in Westport
And I was left with such sweet time
Wondering if between us something
Was deciding to begin or not.

The Banshee's Grotto

After a photograph by Fergus Bourke

'The ... *bean sí** is a solitary being ...'
PATRICIA LYSAGHT

'I heard her across the river crying; a neighbour was dying.'
PADDY O'DONOHUE

'The tear is the anticipation of the eye's future.'
JOSEPH BRODSKY

The messenger comes from that distant place
Beside us where we cannot remember
How unlikely it is that we are here,
Keepers of interiors not our own,
Strangers in whom dawn and twilight are one.

When the black door opens, she often appears,
Keeping her distance from the house of grief,
Circling it with her cry until her tears
Have cut a path to the nerve of a name
That soon will stand alone on a headstone.

* The *bean sí* is the death messenger in the Irish folk tradition.

No one has seen her face or can fathom
Why she comes so far to mourn a stranger.
She is no Rachel weeping for her children,
No Cassandra doomed to remain unheard,
She is the first voice from the other world.

It seems the camera's eye caught her form
Hunched inside a waterfall in Mweelrea.
Is it there she collects tears of delight
Sure that death is bright, or worn down with grief
Must she drink from her Conamara Lethe?

Wind Artist

For Ellen Wingard

Among the kingdom of the winds,
Perhaps, there is one of elegant mind
Who has no need to intrude
On the solitude of single things.

A wind at ease with the depth
Of its own emptiness, who knows
How it was in the beginning,
Before the silence became unbearable
And space rippled to dream things.

A wind who feels how an object strains
To be here, holding its darkness tight
Against the sever of air, ever eager
To enter, and with a swell of light
Dissolve the form in its breathing.

A wind from before memory
Whose patience will see things become
Passionate dust whorled into sighs
Of ghost-song on its wings.

Elemental

Is the word the work
Of someone who tills the blue field,
Unearths its dark plenitude
For the tight seed to release its thought
Into the ferment of clay,
Searching to earth the light
And come to voice in a word of grain
That can sing free in the breeze,
Bathe in the yellow well of the sun,
Avoid the attack of the bird,
And endure the red cell of the oven
Until memory leavens in the gift of bread?

The Pleading

All night long, and all through the white day,
The beat of the wind's bulk against the house,
Pausing only for a breath, and then, again,
The rise and wail of its keening, as if I
Could come out into it, and answer
Its unbearable grief with some sweet name,
From which it could make an antiphon
To calm down its demented legion
Of breezes, or failing that, could I find
And release a granite rock, to open
A duct in the mountain, for it to enter
And search the underworld for itself.

Breakage

Life sentence. First night.
Whistles from cages in Hades.

*

Black dog. He breathes for me.
Nowhere. Dead air.

*

Months later. All normal.
Then, it hit her.

*

Found letters. Too late.
The shock of who she was.

*

Labour pains. Relief.
Then, the child. Damaged.

Inner Circle

For John Moriarty

Stranger sometimes than the yellow crotchet
Of glimpses that civilize the dark, or the
Shelter of voices who stall the dead
Silence that longs to return to stone,
Stranger is the heart, a different scripture,
Weighed down by thoughts of Gods
Who will never emerge, to recommend
One way above another to anywhere,
Lest they distract from the festival
Of vivid presence, where journeys are not
Stretched over distance, and time
Is beyond the fatality of before and
After, and elsewhere and otherwise
Do not intrude on day or night.

Fluent

I would love to live
Like a river flows,
Carried by the surprise
Of its own unfolding.

The Stillness Above is Listening

Rooted in the quiet earth beneath
Which enjoys the quiver as harebells

Relinquish perfect scoops of breeze
Absorbs the syllables when rain lowers

Its silver chorus to coalesce
With granite rocks terse with thirst

And tight with the force of unfreed voice
Feels the moon on its fields brightening

The length of night out into the nowhere
That would love a name like Conamara

The mountain remains a temple of listening
Over years its contours concede to the lonesome

Voices brittle with the threat of what is gathering
Towards their definite houses below

Harvesting the fragments of sound
Into its weight of stillness.

Mountain Christening

For Nöel Hanlon

'Poor wounded name! My bosom
as a bed shall lodge thee.'
SHAKESPEARE

After a hard climb
Through a dry river-bed,
Its scoured stones glistening
Like a white chain to the horizon,
Descending between its links
The long concerto of a stream
Where the listening mountains incline,
Rising against the steep fall of soft bog,
Searching for our grip
In the shimmer of scree.
At last on the summit
Of the Beanna Beola,
Overlooking three valleys,
Delighted to be so high
Above the lives where we dwell,
Together for a while
From other sides of the world,
Sensing each other,

Strangely close, where few reach.
Suddenly, your voice
Calling out my name.
I call yours.
The echoes take us
To the heart of the mountains.
When the silence closes,
You say: Now that they
Have called our names back
The mountains can
Never forget us.

The Night Underneath

Night carries blame for dream and
The other worlds, you become
Mother opening the door to
Walk inside the colour blue
Where animals wear haloes.

Frescoes that evaporate
Into the grey wall of dawn.
You waken to continue on.
Shake yourself free from the night,
Continue with yesterday's life.

Under the day's white surface
All the scripture has withered.
No word, no sound to be heard
In the long wind that reaps dust
From all the harvest of voice.

And the mind behind it all
Has dried up, left nothing but
Its ghost imprint active still
Listening to your footsteps fall,
Their music of red shadows,

Knowing that sooner or later
Some distant light will flicker,
Your blind feet will stumble on
That frail place to send your weight
Through the depth of paper earth.

Imagined Origins

For M

Nothing between us, so near
I hear your skin whisper
What you could never tell
Of the longing that called us.

How through the branches
On to the clay beneath the oak,
A lace of light came down
To wait and watch each day,

And the secrecy of the breeze,
Dying down over the shiver
In the earth, hovering there
To blend its voice to breath,

How, even then, the rain
Through the brow of grasses
Could foreshadow tears
And the trickle of water change,

Or the fright of crows from trees
At dusk into the empty paleness,
This rush of black words today
Searching for you on the white page.

TWO
ENCOUNTERS:
THE ROSARY SONNETS

For Noel Dermot O'Donoghue
And in memory of Pete and Paddy O'Donohue.

ὁ λόγος σὰρξ ἐγένετο

JOHN 1:14

'Love, like fire, can only reveal its brightness
On the failure and the beauty of burnt wood.'

PHILIPPE JACCOTTET

'To stand in the shadow
Of the scar up in the air.'

PAUL CELAN

An Paidrín

I gcuimhne ar Cyril Ó Céirín

Ar nós cheoil na farraige
Tagtha sa bhfoscadh
Ar an teallach

Ag brionglóidí uirthi féin,
An bhrionglóid chéanna
Ó i bhfad i gcéin

Ag snámh go séimh
Idir thrá agus tuile
Na Sé do bheatha, a Mhuire.

The Rosary

As though the music of the ocean
Had come to shelter
On the home hearth

Dreaming of itself
In the selfsame dream
From a far distant region

In buoyant ease
Between the fill and fall
Of waves of Hail Marys.

THE
JOYFUL MYSTERIES

1. The Annunciation

Cast from afar before the stones were born
And rain had rinsed the darkness for colour,
The words have waited for the hunger in her
To become the silence where they could form.

The day's last light frames her by the window,
A young woman with distance in her gaze,
She could never imagine the surprise
That is hovering over her life now.

The sentence awakens like a raven,
Fluttering and dark, opening her heart
To nest the voice that first whispered the earth
From dream into wind, stone, sky and ocean.

She offers to mother the shadow's child;
Her untouched life becoming wild inside.

2. The Visitation

In the morning it takes the mind a while
To find the world again, lost after dream
Has taken the heart to the underworld
To play with the shades of lives not chosen.

She awakens a stranger in her own life,
Her breath loud in the room full of listening.
Taken without touch, her flesh feels the grief
Of belonging to what cannot be seen.

Soon she can no longer bear to be alone.
At dusk she takes the road into the hills.
An anxious moon doubles her among the stone.
A door opens, the older one's eyes fill.

Two women locked in a story of birth.
Each mirrors the secret the other heard.

3. The Nativity

No man reaches where the moon touches a woman.
Even the moon leaves her when she opens
Deeper into the ripple in her womb
That encircles dark to become flesh and bone.

Someone is coming ashore inside her.
A face deciphers itself from water
And she curves around the gathering wave,
Opening to offer the life it craves.

In a corner stall of pilgrim strangers,
She falls and heaves, holding a tide of tears.
A red wire of pain feeds through every vein
Until night unweaves and the child reaches dawn.

Outside each other now, she sees him first.
Flesh of her flesh, her dreamt son safe on earth.

4. The Presentation in the Temple

The words of a secret have rivet eyes
That cannot sleep to forget what they know.
The restrained voice sharpens to an arrow
That will reach its target through any disguise.

Two old people wait in the temple shadows
Where stone and air are hoarsened with prayer
For some door to open in their hunger;
Sometimes children laugh at her twitching nose.

Worn to a thread the old man's rope of days,
Spent unravelling in this empty torment,
Has wizened his silence to words of flint.
When he glimpses the child, his lost voice flares.

His words lodge in the young mother's thought
That a sword of sorrow will pierce her heart.

5. The Finding in the Temple

Oblique to the heart, the word a man seeks
Seldom comes to life in a tongue of flame
From the grate of silence where anger dreams
And stutters in embers thought cannot reach.

When the voice remains fettered, it grows cold
All over the neighbourhood of the word.
In the heart distance cries out to be heard,
When night burns with the face of the beloved.

He is old, yet still betrothed to her dream
That took their home into its possession.
He dwells beside her, anxious and alone.
Hopes when this ends, he will reach her again.

They search the crowd for the child who is gone.
He tells the strangers that it is his son.

THE
SORROWFUL MYSTERIES

6. The Agony in the Garden

Whatever veil of mercy shrouds the dark
Wound that stops weeping in no one, cannot
Stop the torrent of night when it buries thought
And heart beneath the black tears of the earth.

Through scragged bush the moon discovers his face,
Dazed inside the sound of Gethsemane,
Subsiding under the weight of silence
That entombs the cry of his terrified prayer.

What light could endure the dark he entered?
The void that turns the mind into a ruin
Haunted by the tattered screeching of birds
Who nest deep in hunger that mocks all care.

Still he somehow stands in that nothingness;
Raising the chalice of kindness to bless.

7. The Scourging at the Pillar

When we love we love to touch the beloved.
Our hands find joy in the surprise of skin.
Here is where tenderness is uncovered.
Few frontiers hold a world more wondrous in.

Imagine the anger of their disturbance.
They cannot bear the portals his words create.
Helpless, turned inside out by his presence,
Sheltering from themselves as a crowd irate.

Made to face the pillar, the wrists bind him
Under the shadow of the angel of pain,
Who flogs, and waits, prefers a broken rhythm,
Until his back becomes a red text of shame.

His mind holds to the images of those he loves;
While his frightened skin swells under the scourge.

8. The Crowning with Thorns

The thorns woven to your head are nothing
Like the emptiness loosening your mind
From the terse mountains where you served your time
Seeking the hearth in the loneliness of things.

Then that slow glimpse of three faces concresced
In a circle of infinitely gentle gaze
Trusting each thing out of air into form,
Showed you belong to this first tenderness.

You earth divine flame in a young man's frame.
Things rush your senses offering their essence.
Now the earth clenches against you, cold and closed
In a yard forsaken by every name.

On crucifixion duty, bored with routine
The soldiers start mocking and crown you king.

9. The Carrying of the Cross

A kiss on the back of the neck tingles,
Almost sound, a breath of music in bone.
It is here they laid the heavy crossbeam,
Each step a thud inward like sick thunder.

It invades his head. All silence leaves him.
Stooped forward he watches his innocent feet
Search each step for sure ground to take the weight.
He falls face first on the broken pavement.

Those he knows to see will not meet his eyes.
They fear his gaze might unleash misfortune.
Sweat down his back opens a line of wounds.
A white towel absorbs a mirage of his face.

Windows open in the crowd, his heart rends
At the weeping of his mother and friends.

10. The Crucifixion

When at last it comes, it comes in silence;
With no thought for the one to whom it comes,
Or how a heart grieves itself and loved ones
With that last glimpse from its fading presence.

Yet it is intimate, the act of death,
To be so chosen, exposed and taken.
Nowhere untouched. But death wants you broken.
The soldiers must wait ages for your last breath.

With all the bright words, you are found out too,
In agony and terror in vaulted air,
Your mind bleached white by a wind from nowhere
That has waited years for one strike at you.

A slanted rain cuts across the black day.
It turns stones crimson where the cross is laid.

10. The Crucifixion

THE
GLORIOUS MYSTERIES

11. The Resurrection

Oh the rush with which the forgotten mind awakens
Under the day a well of dark where colour dwells
Until it learns the art of light and can reveal,
In neglected things, the freshness thought darkens.

With grey mastery distance starts to blur the horror.
Already the days begin to set around the loss.
The after-silence of his death becomes porous
To the gossip of regret that follows failure.

Through the cold, quiet nighttime of the grave underground,
The earth concentrated on him with complete longing
Until his sleep could recall the dark from beyond
To enfold memory lost in the requiem of mind.

The moon stirs a wave of brightening in the stone.
He rises clothed in the young colours of dawn.

12. The Ascension

With waves the ocean soothes the dark stillness of the shore.
With words the mind would calm the awful, inner quiet.
Offerings to the nothingness on which we trespass.
Our imprint no deeper than breath on a mirror.

Though delighted by the wonder of your return,
To glimpse you is already too much for their eyes.
At your cadence of voice a bird stirs in the heart,
Its wings spread such brightness nothing can hold its form.

You are no longer from here, yet you still linger
In the lightness, wed to the dance you awaken.
As if in drudged-down lives, the song of your new hands
Could raise the soul toward horizons of desire.

You slip through a door of air. Memory comes home,
Bright as a dead tree drawn to blossom by the moon.

13. The Descent of the Holy Spirit

Somewhere in our clay remembers the speed of cold,
Overtaking the surge of colours with grey breath,
And the shudder of fields, as they smother beneath
The white infinity of ice paralysing the world.

How swiftly fear touches this relic-cold in the bone.
After his second going, they hide from the crowd.
Then, like manna from a red wind, a tongue of flame swirls
Into each mind huddled there in the fear-filled room.

The language caul they lived in falls, leaves them wordless,
Then, a kindling, words they never knew they had come
Alive out of nowhere sprung with awakening
That will not cease until winter sets the heart free.

Out in the open now, voices of new belonging,
Needing no courage beyond the fire of their longing.

14. The Assumption

Perhaps time is the keeper of distance and loss,
Knowing that we are but able for a little at a time.
And the innocence of fragments is wise with us,
Keeps us from order that is not native to our dust.

Yet, without warning, a life can suddenly chance
On its hidden rhythm, find a flow it never knew.
Where the heart was blind, subtle worlds rise into view;
Where the mind was forced, crippled thought begins to dance.

As if this day found for her everything she lost,
Her breath infused with harvest she never expected
From the unlived lives she had only touched in dream;
Her mind rests; memory glows in a stairs of twilight.

Her hair kisses the breeze. Her eyes know it is time.
She looks as young as the evening the raven came.

15. The Coronation

It was a long time ago in another land.
Who can tell how it really was before belief
Came toward you with a hunger that could not see you
Except against white air cleansed of the shadow of earth?

No inkling that you were a free spirit who loved
The danger of seeing the world with an open mind,
How you strove to be faithful to uncertainty
And let nothing unquestioned settle in your heart.

You loved to throw caution to the wind when you danced.
To be outside in the dawn before people were,
Letting the blue tides of your dreaming settle ashore.
The village said you put the whole thing into his head.

In the glow of your silence, the heart grows tranquil.
No one will ever know where you had to travel.

THREE
DISTANCES

'The antelope are the only creatures swift
enough to catch the distance.'

LOUISE ERDRICH

'Every thought should recall the
ruin of a smile.'

E. M. CIORAN

'Because the outer walls of God are glass.'

ANNE CARSON

Words

For Ethel and Sheila

Words may know the way to reach the dark
Where the wild sweetness of a hillside
Is distilled in a hive under grass.

Words may tell how the rhythm of tide
Can soften its salt-voice on the shore
Through music it steals when stone confides.

Words may capture how the ravens soar
In silk black selves far into the blue
To seek the nest of night's colour hoard.

Words may live under ground out of view
Holding a vanished world etched in scrolls
Under sands where streets lay and youth grew.

When the red vapour breathes through the soul
And pain closes down the ease of the day
Words stagger back to silence and fold.

Wings

For Josie

Whenever a goose was killed,
My mother got the two wings.
They were placed on the rack
Over the black Stanley range
And taken down to sweep
Around the grate and the floor.

Local women said: no matter
How you sprinkled it, every time
You'd sweep a concrete floor,
You'd get more off it.
As if, deep down,
There was only dust.

Often during sweeping,
A ray of light
Through the window
Would reveal
How empty air
Could hold a wall
Of drunken dust.

Instead of being folded around
Each side of a living body,
Embracing the warmth
And urgency of a beating heart,
The wings are broken objects now,
Rubbed and rubbed, edge down
Into an insatiable floor,
Smothered and thinned,
Until they become ghost feathers
Around a cusp of bone
Polished by motherly hand.

Never again to be disturbed
Every year by the call
Of the wild geese overhead,
Reminding them of the sky,
Urging them to raise the life
They embrace, to climb the breeze
Beyond the farm, towards horizons
That veil the green surge of the ocean.

The Transparent Border

There is a strange edge to the wind today,
Some irritation with the patient strain
Of trees, the 'willing to bend with anything'
Trick of the rushes, the shoals of shadow
Perplexing the lake and all the silent
Aloofness of the stones, something
Very old, perhaps, resentment towards
These bog fields, each rooted in its dark
Continuum and known to people by name
And season, from which many stones
Have been claimed to make houses
Where they grow warm with human echoes,
And the lake, to which the mountains come
To mirror themselves, where twilights linger
Before night sends everything to rest;
A resentment at the way they all somehow
Slipped across the transparent border
From idea into individual thing,
Glistening with name, colour and form
At the beginning, when the wind would have
Felt breath was where presence lived.

The Angel of the Bog

For Lelia

The angel of the bog mourns in the wind
That loiters all over these black meadows.
Remembers how it chose branches to strum
From the orchestra of trees that stood here;
How at twilight a chorus of birds came
To silence in nests of darkening air.

Raindrops filter through leaves, silver the air,
Wash off the film of dust to release nets
Of fragrance on which the wind can sweeten
Before expiring among the debris
That brightens each year with fallen colour
Before the weight of winter seals the ground.

The dark eyes of the angel of the bog
Never open now when dawn comes to dress
The famished grass with splendid veils of red,
Amber, white, as if its soul were urgent
And young with possibility and dreams
That a vanished life might become visible.

Placenta

For Máire Bheag

It grew between you
Naturally.
This wise wall
That took everything
From you
He needed.

Grew varicose,
To carry through
The seepage of calcium.
Holding rhythm,
Offering time,
To structure and settle
The white scribble
Until it finds
The stillness
And strength
Of bone.

Fed the beat
Of your pulse
Through the dark,
A first music,
To steady the quiver

That would become
His heart.

Sieved from the stream
Of your breathing,
The breath of trees,
Fragrance of flowers,
The heavy scent of woman,
Chorus of seas,
Ripples of the ancestral,
And the strange taste
Of a shadow-father,
When you kissed.

Feels toward the end
The temper of flow change
And absorbs the white stream
To urge the child free.

On your own,
Now,
Growing away
From each other.
Nothing
Between you
But the distance
That will remain
Alive
With invisible tissue.

Mountain-Looking

For the Burren Action Group

who saved Mullach Mór

The mountain waits for no one
But rises on its own to overlook

The blind spread of fields and
The local pride of trees adept
At the art of singular ascent.

The lakes which stay in place,
Somehow held up by the threaded
Resolve of the bog that rusts the water
Until it takes dark for depth.

The grey certainty of the stones,
Stained yellow with moss and lichen,
Who serve as sentinels among the bushes,
Alert for the whisper of the ice
That will return to retrieve them
In white nests from the loose air.

And the earth-orphans
In their strong homes
That light up at night

On sealed ground
Where they shelter from
The seamless totality of the dark
Claiming all the spaces of separation.

Watched by animals,
They emerge at daytime;
No surface here
Could wear frowns
Like these faces.
Their limbs and eyes
Blurred with desire,
They climb up sometimes,
Hoping, maybe,
To see what the summit sees.

Seduced?

In the empty carton
Inside the door of the attic,
Five blue crystals wait
To entice the visitors
Who will come in the dark,
Breath seduced
By the distant scent
Of such blue delight.

Frost and hunger
Will bring them in
To the labyrinth
Of breathing spaces
That run through
The stone walls.

They will never see
How beautiful
The walls are on
The other side, the warm
Surfaces of soft peach
That shelter the joy
Of love, music and thought,

With windows toward
Mountains adored by light.

While you sleep,
They will feast
In the dark,
Lick and chew
Each minuscule fibre
Of the forbidden food,
Replace the blue
With emptiness.

By the time
Thirst takes them,
Desperately,
Down to the lake
It will already
Be too late.

At the Edge

Sometimes, behind the lines
Of words giving voice to the blue wind
That blows across the amber fields
Of your years, whispering the hungers
Your dignity conceals, and the caves
Of loss opening along shores forgotten
By the ocean, you almost hear the depth
Of white silence, rising to deny everything.

Breakage

Has to. Crack. Wet street.
Her first car stops.

~

His children's eyes. Can't meet his.
Old folks' home.

~

Said why. Wrote name with care: Susan.
Then did it.

~

No sleep. The voices own you.
They take you with them.

~

If she knew, she'd go. But she doesn't.
Happy.

Double Exposure

Sometimes you see us
Run into each other in a place
Where we cannot simply pass,
Say at a party, and you overhear
Our breath quiveringly collect
To shape a voice sure enough
To play out some pleasantry;
Something humorous is preferable,
It covers perfectly and shows
That everything is as it should be.
As smoothly as possible
We allow ourselves to be waylaid
By some other conversation and escape.
Though we move around the room,
We always know where we stand,
Still strangely bound to each other
In this intermittent dance
Between the music, each careful
To hold up the other side of all
We were to each other before
It stopped, and let nothing drop
From the invisible ruin
We carry between us.

Elemental

Is the word the work
Of some elder who quarries
The green mountain
For the hard deposit,
Refines it under black dust
That a bellows blows red,
Hammers it to a wafer
On the white anvil
Until it can carry its own loss,
The anger of the withering fire,
The unstruck echo of the mountain,
Yet succumb to breath
Like pollen to the breeze?

The Night

1 February 1994

Nothing can make the night stay outside,
It pours in everywhere, smothers my room
With black air prepared in some unseen cave,
Tightens around my skull the root silence
Of that room in rock; nothing broke the dark
Except the tick of raindrops from above;
Centuries seeping through the limestone
To point a cold finger of stalactite
At emptiness never softened by breath;
Where the sore of absence was never felt
In cold that fasted solid from light,
A hermit space that let in no question.
This dark is all eyes; but cannot feel
How it blackens the breath and the heart.
It weighs me down as it would a stone.

AUTHOR'S
NOTES

The author wishes to acknowledge the following publications in which earlier versions of some of these poems appeared: *Lapis*, *The Connacht Tribune*, *The Whoseday Book*, *Ireland of the Welcomes*, *Departures*.

Lines from Naomi Shihab Nye's poem 'Adios', from *Words under the Words: Selected Poems* (Far Corner Books, Portland, Oregon, 1995), are reprinted by permission.

p. 22   This poem takes its title from the title of a photograph by the Conamara photographer Fergus Bourke.

The authoritative work on the Banshee tradition in Irish folklore is Patricia Lysaght's *The Banshee* (Roberts Rinehart, 1996).

p. 27   The rosary is a form of devotion accompanying the contemplation of fifteen mysteries highlighted from the life of Jesus. They are divided into the Joyful, Sorrowful and Glorious Mysteries. Fifteen decades of Hail Marys are recited; each decade is preceded by an Our Father and followed by a Glory be to the Father. This devotion is usually prayed on rosary beads, consisting of a sequence of beads which represent the five decades corresponding to one set of the mysteries. According to the theologian Noel Dermot

O'Donoghue, the rosary enfolds the mystical heart of Christianity. The name 'rosary' comes from the flower, the rose, which in the medieval period was understood as a symbol of life eternal. The rosary in its present form emerged in late medieval Christianity.

p. 40   This poem was first written in Irish and 'The Rosary' is the English translation.

p. 76   Mullach Mór is a spectacular mountain in the Burren in the West of Ireland. It has been the subject of a recently successful ten-year environmental campaign by the Burren Action Group to prevent the Irish government from building an interpretation centre for tourists there.

p. 91   Corcomroe is the ruin of a twelfth-century Cistercian monastery in the Burren. It was dedicated to Maria de Petra Fertilis: Mary of the Fertile Rock.

JOHN O'DONOHUE wrote a number of international bestsellers, including *Anam Cara*, *Eternal Echoes*, *Divine Beauty* and *Benedictus*. He also wrote *Person als Vermittlung* on the philosophy of Hegel and two collections of poetry, *Echoes of Memory* and *Conamara Blues*.